Sweet Harmony

A Peach Jam Adventure

SWEET HARMONY

First edition. February 5, 2024.

ISBN: 979-8224439720

Written by Jose Maria.

Table of Contents

Jose Maria

❖ Introduction

A. Welcome and Brief Overview

Welcome to the delightful world of peach jam-making! In this culinary adventure, we'll explore the art of preserving peaches, transforming their natural sweetness into jars of golden goodness. Whether you're a seasoned jam enthusiast or a beginner in the world of preserving, this journey promises a symphony of flavors and the joy of crafting your own peachy creations.

B. The Joy of Preserving Peaches

There's something magical about capturing the essence of ripe, juicy peaches in a jar. Preserving peaches not only allows you to savor their vibrant taste throughout the year but also brings a sense of nostalgia and tradition to your kitchen. As we embark on this peach jam adventure, let's celebrate the joy of preserving, creating, and sharing these delightful gems with loved ones.

C. Essential Tools and Ingredients

Before we dive into the world of peach jam, let's ensure we have the right tools and ingredients to make this experience smooth and enjoyable. Here's a quick checklist:

Tools:

- Large Pot: For cooking and simmering the jam.
- Canning Jars with Lids: To store your peachy creations.
- Canning Funnel: Ensures mess-free jar filling.
- Jar Lifter: Safely handles hot jars.
- Citrus Juicer: For added flavor, if needed.
- Pectin Thermometer: Monitors jam consistency.

Ingredients:

1. Fresh Peaches: Select ripe, fragrant peaches for the best flavor.

2. Granulated Sugar: Provides sweetness and aids in preservation.
3. Lemon Juice: Enhances the natural flavor and acts as a natural preservative.
4. Pectin: A natural thickening agent for achieving the desired jam consistency.
5. Spices and Flavor Enhancers: Customize with vanilla, cinnamon, or other preferred additions.

Now that we're equipped, let's move on to the next step: selecting the perfect peaches for our peach jam masterpiece!

Chapter (1) Getting Started with Peach Jam

A. Selecting the Perfect Peaches

Choosing the right peaches lays the foundation for a delectable jam. Follow these tips for selecting the perfect peaches:

1. Ripe and Fragrant: Opt for peaches with a sweet aroma, indicating ripeness.
2. Firmness: Select peaches that yield slightly to gentle pressure without being mushy.
3. Color: Look for vibrant, golden-yellow peaches with minimal green undertones.
4. Uniformity: Choose peaches that are uniformly colored and free from bruises or blemishes.

B. Washing, Peeling, and Pitting Techniques

Now that you have your peaches, let's prepare them for jam-making:

1. Washing: Rinse peaches under cool running water to remove any dirt or debris. Gently pat them dry with a clean kitchen towel.
2. Peeling: To easily peel peaches, make a small "X" at the base of each peach, then blanch them in boiling water for about 30 seconds. Transfer to an ice bath, and the skins should peel off easily.
3. Pitting: Cut the peaches in half and remove the pit. For easy slicing, consider a peach pitter or simply twist the halves in opposite directions to separate.

C. Understanding Pectin and Sweeteners

Understanding the role of pectin and sweeteners is crucial for achieving the perfect jam consistency:

1. Pectin: Pectin is a natural substance found in fruits that, when cooked, causes jams to gel. Some fruits, like apples and citrus, have high natural pectin levels. Additional pectin may be needed for low-pectin fruits like peaches. Choose between powdered or liquid pectin based on your preference and recipe.
2. Sweeteners: Granulated sugar is commonly used in jam-making for sweetness and preservation. The ratio of sugar to fruit varies in recipes. Low-sugar options are available, but sugar plays a role in both flavor and texture, so adjustments should be made cautiously.

Armed with the perfect peaches and essential knowledge, let's proceed to the heart of our adventure: crafting delicious peach jams! Choose a basic peach jam recipe from Section III, and we'll dive into the sweet symphony of flavors.

Chapter (2) Basic Peach Jam Recipes

A. Classic Peach Jam
Ingredients:

- 4 cups peeled, pitted, and finely chopped ripe peaches
- 5 cups granulated sugar
- 1/4 cup lemon juice
- 1 package (1.75 oz) powdered fruit pectin

Instructions:

1. In a large pot, combine chopped peaches, lemon juice, and pectin. Stir well to mix.
2. Bring the mixture to a boil over medium-high heat, stirring constantly.
3. Once boiling, add the sugar all at once. Stirring constantly, return the mixture to a rapid boil that cannot be stirred down.
4. Boil for 1-2 minutes, or until the desired consistency is reached. Skim off any foam.
5. Remove the pot from heat and let it sit for 5 minutes. Stir gently to distribute the fruit.
6. Ladle the hot jam into sterilized jars, leaving about 1/4-inch headspace. Wipe the jar rims and place sterilized lids on jars.
7. Process in a boiling water bath for 10 minutes. Allow jars to cool on a clean towel or cooling rack.

B. Peach Vanilla Jam

Ingredients:

- 4 cups peeled, pitted, and finely chopped ripe peaches
- 1 vanilla bean, split and seeds scraped
- 5 cups granulated sugar
- 1/4 cup lemon juice
- 1 package (1.75 oz) powdered fruit pectin

Instructions:

1. Follow the same instructions as for Classic Peach Jam, adding the scraped vanilla seeds along with the lemon juice and pectin.

C. Low-Sugar Peach Jam

Ingredients:

- 4 cups peeled, pitted, and finely chopped ripe peaches
- 3 cups granulated sugar
- 1/4 cup lemon juice
- 1 package (1.75 oz) low-sugar powdered fruit pectin

Instructions:

1. Combine peaches, lemon juice, and pectin in a pot, stirring well.
2. Bring the mixture to a boil over medium-high heat.
3. Add the sugar all at once, stirring constantly, and return to a rapid boil.
4. Boil for 1-2 minutes until the jam thickens.
5. Follow steps 5-7 from the Classic Peach Jam recipe for jarring and processing.

D. Spiced Peach Jam

Ingredients:

- 4 cups peeled, pitted, and finely chopped ripe peaches
- 5 cups granulated sugar
- 1/4 cup lemon juice
- 1 package (1.75 oz) powdered fruit pectin
- 1 teaspoon ground cinnamon
- 1/2 teaspoon ground nutmeg

Instructions:

1. Follow the same instructions as for Classic Peach Jam, adding the ground cinnamon and nutmeg along with the lemon juice and pectin.

Choose your favorite basic peach jam recipe, and let the aroma of simmering peaches fill your kitchen with anticipation. Once you've mastered the basics, we can explore creative variations in Section IV!

Chapter (3) Beyond the Basics: Creative Peach Jam Variations

A. Peach and Basil Jam
Ingredients:

- 4 cups peeled, pitted, and finely chopped ripe peaches
- 5 cups granulated sugar
- 1/4 cup lemon juice
- 1 package (1.75 oz) powdered fruit pectin
- 1/2 cup fresh basil leaves, finely chopped

Instructions:

1. Follow the same instructions as for Classic Peach Jam, adding the chopped basil along with the lemon juice and pectin.

B. Ginger-Peach Jam
Ingredients:

- 4 cups peeled, pitted, and finely chopped ripe peaches
- 5 cups granulated sugar
- 1/4 cup lemon juice
- 1 package (1.75 oz) powdered fruit pectin
- 2 tablespoons fresh ginger, finely grated

Instructions:

1. Follow the same instructions as for Classic Peach Jam, adding the grated ginger along with the lemon juice and pectin.

C. Bourbon-Infused Peach Jam
Ingredients:

- 4 cups peeled, pitted, and finely chopped ripe peaches
- 5 cups granulated sugar
- 1/4 cup lemon juice
- 1 package (1.75 oz) powdered fruit pectin
- 1/4 cup bourbon

Instructions:

1. Follow the same instructions as for Classic Peach Jam, adding the bourbon along with the lemon juice and pectin. Stir well.

D. Berry-Peach Fusion Jam
Ingredients:

- 2 cups peeled, pitted, and finely chopped ripe peaches
- 2 cups mixed berries (strawberries, raspberries, or blackberries)
- 5 cups granulated sugar
- 1/4 cup lemon juice
- 1 package (1.75 oz) powdered fruit pectin

Instructions:

1. In a large pot, combine peaches, mixed berries, lemon juice, and pectin. Stir well to mix.
2. Bring the mixture to a boil over medium-high heat, stirring constantly.
3. Once boiling, add the sugar all at once. Stirring constantly, return the mixture to a rapid boil that cannot be stirred down.
4. Boil for 1-2 minutes, or until the desired consistency is reached. Skim off any foam.
5. Follow steps 5-7 from the Classic Peach Jam recipe for jarring

and processing.

Choose a creative peach jam variation that intrigues your taste buds, and let the fusion of unique flavors elevate your jam-making experience! If you have a preference, or if you'd like more options, feel free to let me know.

Chapter (4) International Flair: Peach Jam Inspired by Global Cuisines

A. Mediterranean Peach Jam with Citrus
  Ingredients:

- 4 cups peeled, pitted, and finely chopped ripe peaches
- 5 cups granulated sugar
- 1/4 cup lemon juice
- 1 package (1.75 oz) powdered fruit pectin
- Zest of one orange
- Zest of one lemon

Instructions:

1. Follow the same instructions as for Classic Peach Jam, adding the orange and lemon zest along with the lemon juice and pectin.

B. Asian-Inspired Ginger-Peach Chutney
Ingredients:

- 4 cups peeled, pitted, and finely chopped ripe peaches
- 1 cup brown sugar
- 1/4 cup rice vinegar
- 2 tablespoons fresh ginger, finely grated
- 1 teaspoon soy sauce
- 1/2 teaspoon red pepper flakes (adjust to taste)

Instructions:

1. In a pot, combine peaches, brown sugar, rice vinegar, ginger, soy sauce, and red pepper flakes. Stir well.

2. Bring the mixture to a simmer over medium heat, stirring occasionally.
3. Simmer for 20-25 minutes or until the chutney thickens. Stir frequently.
4. Adjust sweetness and spice according to taste.
5. Once the chutney reaches the desired consistency, let it cool before transferring to sterilized jars.

C. Tropical Peach Jam with Coconut
Ingredients:

- 4 cups peeled, pitted, and finely chopped ripe peaches
- 5 cups granulated sugar
- 1/4 cup lemon juice
- 1 package (1.75 oz) powdered fruit pectin
- 1 cup shredded coconut

Instructions

1. Follow the same instructions as for Classic Peach Jam, adding the shredded coconut along with the lemon juice and pectin.

Choose an international-inspired peach jam that transports your taste buds to new culinary heights! If you have a preference or would like more options, feel free to let me know. Happy jam-making!

Chapter (5) Holiday Extravaganza: Peach Jam Festive Favorites

A. Thanksgiving Peach Jam Cranberry Sauce
Ingredients:

- 1 cup fresh cranberries
- 1 cup sugar
- 1/2 cup water
- 1/4 cup peach jam
- Zest and juice of one orange
- 1 cinnamon stick

Instructions:

1. In a saucepan, combine cranberries, sugar, water, peach jam, orange zest, orange juice, and a cinnamon stick.
2. Bring the mixture to a boil, then reduce heat and simmer until cranberries burst and the sauce thickens.
3. Remove from heat and let it cool before serving as a sweet and tangy cranberry sauce for Thanksgiving.

B. Christmas Spiced Peach Jam Cookies
Ingredients:

- 1 cup unsalted butter, softened
- 1 cup sugar
- 2 large eggs
- 1 teaspoon vanilla extract
- 3 cups all-purpose flour
- 1 teaspoon baking powder
- 1/2 teaspoon salt
- 1/2 cup peach jam

- 1 teaspoon ground cinnamon
- Powdered sugar for dusting (optional)

Instructions:

1. Preheat oven to 350°F (175°C) and line baking sheets with parchment paper.
2. In a large bowl, cream together butter and sugar until light and fluffy.
3. Beat in eggs one at a time, then add vanilla extract.
4. In a separate bowl, whisk together flour, baking powder, and salt.
5. Gradually add the dry ingredients to the wet ingredients, mixing until combined.
6. Fold in peach jam and ground cinnamon.
7. Drop rounded tablespoons of dough onto the prepared baking sheets.
8. Bake for 10-12 minutes or until the edges are lightly golden.
9. Allow the cookies to cool on the baking sheets for a few minutes before transferring to a wire rack.
10. Dust with powdered sugar if desired.

C. New Year's Eve Peach Jam Champagne Toasts
Ingredients:

- Champagne or sparkling wine
- Peach jam
- Fresh peach slices for garnish

Instructions:

1. Place a small spoonful of peach jam at the bottom of each champagne flute.
2. Pour chilled champagne or sparkling wine over the peach jam.

3. Gently stir to mix the peach jam into the bubbly.
4. Garnish with a slice of fresh peach on the rim.
5. Toast to the New Year with this delightful and effervescent peach jam champagne.

Chapter (6) Savory and Spicy Peach Jam Creations

A. Jalapeño Peach Jam
Ingredients:

- 4 cups peeled, pitted, and finely chopped ripe peaches
- 3 cups granulated sugar
- 1/4 cup lemon juice
- 1 package (1.75 oz) powdered fruit pectin
- 2-3 jalapeños, seeds removed and finely chopped

Instructions:

1. In a large pot, combine peaches, sugar, lemon juice, and pectin. Stir well.
2. Bring the mixture to a boil over medium-high heat, stirring constantly.
3. Add the chopped jalapeños and continue to boil for 1-2 minutes until the jam thickens.
4. Skim off any foam and proceed with jarring as per the Classic Peach Jam recipe.

B. Rosemary Peach Jam
Ingredients:

- 4 cups peeled, pitted, and finely chopped ripe peaches
- 5 cups granulated sugar
- 1/4 cup lemon juice
- 1 package (1.75 oz) powdered fruit pectin
- 2 tablespoons fresh rosemary, finely chopped

Instructions:

1. Follow the same instructions as for Classic Peach Jam, adding the chopped rosemary along with the lemon juice and pectin.

C. Balsamic Peach Jam
Ingredients:

- 4 cups peeled, pitted, and finely chopped ripe peaches
- 1 cup granulated sugar
- 1/2 cup balsamic vinegar
- 1/4 cup lemon juice
- 1 package (1.75 oz) powdered fruit pectin

Instructions:

1. In a pot, combine peaches, sugar, balsamic vinegar, lemon juice, and pectin. Stir well.
2. Bring the mixture to a simmer over medium heat, stirring frequently.
3. Simmer for 15-20 minutes or until the jam thickens to your liking.
4. Follow steps 5-7 from the Classic Peach Jam recipe for jarring and processing.

Savor the delightful balance of sweet, savory, and spicy with these unique peach jam creations. If you have a preference or need more options, feel free to let me know! Enjoy the journey of experimenting with flavors.

Chapter (7) Sweet Endings: Peach Jam Desserts

A. Peach Jam-Filled Thumbprint Cookies

Ingredients:

- 1 cup unsalted butter, softened
- 1/2 cup granulated sugar
- 2 large egg yolks
- 2 teaspoons vanilla extract
- 2 cups all-purpose flour
- 1/2 teaspoon salt
- Peach jam for filling

Instructions:

1. Preheat your oven to 350°F (175°C) and line baking sheets with parchment paper.
2. In a large bowl, cream together the butter and sugar until light and fluffy.
3. Beat in the egg yolks and vanilla extract until well combined.
4. In a separate bowl, whisk together the flour and salt. Gradually add this to the butter mixture, mixing until just combined.
5. Roll the dough into small balls and place them on the prepared baking sheets.
6. Make an indentation in the center of each cookie using your thumb or the back of a teaspoon.
7. Fill each indentation with a small spoonful of peach jam.
8. Bake for 10-12 minutes or until the edges are lightly golden.
9. Allow the cookies to cool on the baking sheets for a few minutes before transferring them to a wire rack to cool completely.

B. Peach Jam Swirl Ice Cream

Ingredients:

- 2 cups heavy cream
- 1 cup whole milk
- 3/4 cup granulated sugar
- 1 tablespoon pure vanilla extract
- 1 cup peach jam

Instructions:

1. In a mixing bowl, whisk together the heavy cream, whole milk, sugar, and vanilla extract until the sugar is dissolved.
2. Pour the mixture into an ice cream maker and churn according to the manufacturer's instructions.
3. In the last few minutes of churning, add spoonfuls of peach jam to create a swirl effect.
4. Transfer the churned ice cream to a lidded container and freeze for at least 4 hours or until firm.

C. Peach Jam Cheesecake Bars

Ingredients:

- 2 cups graham cracker crumbs
- 1/2 cup unsalted butter, melted
- 16 oz cream cheese, softened
- 1 cup granulated sugar
- 3 large eggs
- 1 teaspoon vanilla extract
- 1 cup peach jam

Instructions:

1. Preheat your oven to 325°F (160°C) and line a baking dish with parchment paper.

2. In a bowl, combine graham cracker crumbs and melted butter. Press the mixture into the bottom of the prepared dish to form the crust.

3. In another bowl, beat together the cream cheese and sugar until smooth.

4. Add the eggs one at a time, beating well after each addition. Stir in the vanilla extract.

5. Pour the cream cheese mixture over the crust and smooth the top.

6. Drop spoonfuls of peach jam onto the cream cheese mixture and swirl with a knife for a marbled effect.

7. Bake for 35-40 minutes or until the edges are set, and the center is slightly jiggly.

8. Allow the cheesecake bars to cool in the pan before refrigerating for at least 4 hours or overnight.

9. Once chilled, lift the parchment paper to remove the bars from the pan and cut into squares.

Indulge in these sweet peach jam-infused desserts for a delightful ending to your peachy culinary journey. If you have a preference or need more dessert options, feel free to let me know! Enjoy these scrumptious treats.

Chapter (8) Homemade Gifts with Peach Jam

A. DIY Peach Jam Gift Baskets
Materials:

- Jars of assorted peach jams
- Baskets or gift boxes
- Decorative tissue paper
- Ribbon or twine
- Small tags or cards

Instructions:

1. Arrange jars of peach jam in the basket or gift box.
2. Add some decorative tissue paper to create a colorful base.
3. Tie a ribbon or twine around the basket or box, securing the jars in place.
4. Attach a small tag or card with a heartfelt message or a list of the jam varieties included.
5. Consider adding complementary items such as homemade cookies, crackers, or a small cheese selection for a complete gift.

B. Creative Packaging Ideas
Materials:

- Clear glass jars with lids
- Fabric or patterned paper
- Rubber bands or twine
- Gift tags or labels
- Adhesive glue or double-sided tape

Instructions:

1. Cut fabric or patterned paper into squares large enough to cover the jar lids.
2. Secure the fabric or paper to the lid using a rubber band or twine, creating a rustic look.
3. Attach a gift tag or label with the jam flavor and a personal message.
4. Consider placing the jar in a small burlap or organza bag for an added touch.

C. Personalized Jam Jar Labels
Materials:

- Printable label sheets or plain paper
- Color printer
- Scissors or a label cutter
- Clear adhesive book cover or laminating sheets (optional)

Instructions:

1. Design personalized labels using a graphic design tool or a template.
2. Print the labels on a color printer.
3. Cut out the labels, leaving a small border for easy attachment.
4. Optionally, cover the labels with clear adhesive book cover or laminating sheets for durability.
5. Attach the labels to the jars, making sure they are secure and centered.

Whether you're creating delightful gift baskets, adding a touch of creativity to the packaging, or personalizing labels for your peach jams, these DIY ideas will turn your homemade treats into memorable and heartfelt gifts. If you have specific preferences or need more ideas, feel free to let me know! Happy gifting!

Chapter (9) Troubleshooting Tips and FAQs

A. Common Jam-Making Pitfalls

Jam Too Runny:

Possible Causes: Insufficient cooking time, not enough pectin, or not reaching the right temperature.

Solution: Return the jam to a boil and continue cooking, adding more pectin if needed.

Jam Too Thick:

Possible Causes: Overcooking or using too much pectin.

Solution: Adjust consistency by adding water or fruit juice, and adjust future recipes accordingly.

Fruit Floating to the Top:

Possible Causes: Not stirring the jam before filling jars or using overly ripe fruit.

Solution: Stir the jam gently before filling jars and use slightly underripe fruit.

Jars Not Sealing Properly:

Possible Causes: Inadequate processing time, improper sealing technique, or damaged jar rims.

Solution: Re-process jars with new lids or store unsealed jars in the refrigerator.

B. Troubleshooting Guide

Jam Won't Set:

Possible Causes: Not enough pectin, undercooking, or inaccurate measurements.

Solution: Add more pectin or cook the jam longer. Use accurate measurements for consistent results.

Foaming During Cooking:

Possible Causes: Using too high heat or adding fruit too quickly.

Solution: Reduce heat and add fruit gradually. Skim off foam as needed during cooking.

Jars Leaking Liquid:

Possible Causes: Incorrect headspace, not wiping jar rims, or faulty lids.

Solution: Ensure proper headspace, wipe rims, and use new, undamaged lids.

C. Frequently Asked Questions

Can I use frozen peaches for jam?

Answer: Yes, frozen peaches can be used. Thaw and drain excess liquid before proceeding with the recipe.

How long does peach jam last?

Answer: Properly processed and sealed peach jam can last up to a year in a cool, dark place. Once opened, store in the refrigerator for up to a month.

Can I reduce the sugar in jam recipes?

Answer: Yes, but it may affect the taste, texture, and shelf life. Consider using low-sugar pectin or recipes designed for reduced sugar.

Why did my jam crystallize?

Answer: Overcooking or using too much sugar can cause crystallization. Follow recommended cooking times and sugar ratios.

Feel free to troubleshoot based on these tips, and if you have specific questions or encounter unique challenges, don't hesitate to ask for assistance! Happy jam-making!

Chapter (10) Breakfast Delights: Peach Jam in the Morning

A. Peach Jam-Filled Pancakes

Ingredients:

- 1 cup all-purpose flour
- 2 tablespoons granulated sugar
- 1 teaspoon baking powder
- 1/2 teaspoon baking soda
- 1/4 teaspoon salt
- 1 cup buttermilk
- 1 large egg
- 2 tablespoons unsalted butter, melted
- Peach jam for filling
- Butter or oil for cooking

Instructions:

1. In a bowl, whisk together the flour, sugar, baking powder, baking soda, and salt.
2. In another bowl, whisk together the buttermilk, egg, and melted butter.
3. Pour the wet ingredients into the dry ingredients and stir until just combined.
4. Heat a griddle or non-stick skillet over medium heat and lightly grease with butter or oil.
5. Pour 1/4 cup of batter onto the griddle for each pancake.
6. Once bubbles form on the surface, add a spoonful of peach jam in the center and top with a little more batter to cover.
7. Flip the pancakes when the edges start to set and cook until golden brown on both sides.

8. Serve warm with a dollop of peach jam on top.

B. Peach Jam-Stuffed French Toast
Ingredients:

- 4 slices thick-cut bread
- 2 large eggs
- 1/2 cup milk
- 1 teaspoon vanilla extract
- Butter for cooking
- Peach jam for stuffing
- Powdered sugar for dusting (optional)
- Maple syrup for serving

Instructions:

1. In a shallow bowl, whisk together the eggs, milk, and vanilla extract.
2. Spread a generous amount of peach jam on two slices of bread and top with the remaining slices, creating sandwiches.
3. Heat a skillet over medium heat and melt a tablespoon of butter.
4. Dip each sandwich into the egg mixture, coating both sides.
5. Cook the sandwiches on the skillet until golden brown on both sides.
6. Dust with powdered sugar if desired and serve with maple syrup.

C. Peach Jam Breakfast Parfait
Ingredients:

- Greek yogurt

- Granola
- Fresh sliced peaches
- Peach jam
- Honey (optional)

Instructions:

1. In a glass or bowl, layer Greek yogurt, granola, and fresh sliced peaches.
2. Add a spoonful of peach jam on top of each layer.
3. Repeat the layers until the glass is filled.
4. Drizzle with honey if desired.
5. Serve immediately and enjoy the delightful combination of flavors.

These breakfast delights with peach jam will add a burst of flavor to your morning routine. Whether you prefer pancakes, French toast, or a yogurt parfait, the sweet and tangy notes of peach jam will make your breakfast extra special. If you have a preference or need more breakfast ideas, feel free to let me know!

Chapter (11) Quick and Easy Peach Jam Snacks

A. Peach Jam and Cream Cheese Bagel Bites
Ingredients:

- Mini bagels, halved and toasted
- Cream cheese
- Peach jam
- Fresh mint leaves for garnish

Instructions:

1. Spread a layer of cream cheese on each toasted bagel half.
2. Spoon a small amount of peach jam on top of the cream cheese.
3. Garnish with fresh mint leaves.
4. Serve as a delightful bite-sized snack.

B. Peach Jam Glazed Nuts
Ingredients:

- 2 cups mixed nuts (almonds, walnuts, pecans)
- 1/4 cup peach jam
- 2 tablespoons butter, melted
- 1 tablespoon brown sugar
- 1/2 teaspoon cinnamon
- Pinch of salt

Instructions:

1. Preheat the oven to 350°F (175°C) and line a baking sheet with parchment paper.
2. In a bowl, mix together peach jam, melted butter, brown sugar,

cinnamon, and a pinch of salt.

3. Add the mixed nuts to the bowl, tossing to coat them evenly with the peach jam mixture.
4. Spread the coated nuts onto the prepared baking sheet in a single layer.
5. Bake for 15-20 minutes, stirring occasionally, until the nuts are golden and glazed.
6. Allow the nuts to cool before serving.

C. Peach Jam Bruschetta
Ingredients:

- Baguette, sliced
- Goat cheese
- Peach jam
- Fresh basil leaves
- Balsamic glaze for drizzling

Instructions:

1. Toast the baguette slices until they are lightly crispy.
2. Spread a layer of goat cheese on each toasted baguette slice.
3. Spoon a small amount of peach jam on top of the goat cheese.
4. Garnish with fresh basil leaves.
5. Drizzle with balsamic glaze for an extra burst of flavor.
6. Serve as a quick and elegant bruschetta snack.

These quick and easy peach jam snacks offer a delightful combination of flavors and textures, perfect for a midday pick-me-up or an appetizer for gatherings. If you have a preference or need more snack ideas, feel free to let me know! Enjoy these tasty bites.

Chapter (12) Refreshing Beverages with Peach Jam

A. Peach Jam Lemonade
Ingredients:

- 1 cup freshly squeezed lemon juice
- 1/2 cup peach jam
- 1/2 cup granulated sugar (adjust to taste)
- 4 cups cold water
- Ice cubes
- Lemon slices and mint leaves for garnish

Instructions:

1. In a pitcher, combine freshly squeezed lemon juice, peach jam, and granulated sugar. Stir until the sugar is dissolved.
2. Add cold water to the pitcher and mix well.
3. Taste and adjust the sweetness by adding more sugar if needed.
4. Refrigerate until ready to serve.
5. Serve over ice and garnish with lemon slices and fresh mint leaves.

B. Sparkling Peach Jam Spritzer
Ingredients:

- 1/4 cup peach jam
- 1 cup sparkling water
- 1 tablespoon freshly squeezed lime juice
- Ice cubes
- Mint sprigs for garnish

Instructions:

1. In a glass, spoon peach jam at the bottom.
2. Add sparkling water and stir until the jam is dissolved.
3. Squeeze fresh lime juice into the mixture and stir again.
4. Add ice cubes to the glass.
5. Garnish with mint sprigs and enjoy this sparkling and peachy spritzer.

C. Peach Jam Smoothie
Ingredients:

- 1 cup frozen peach slices
- 1/2 banana
- 1/2 cup Greek yogurt
- 1/4 cup peach jam
- 1/2 cup almond milk (or your preferred milk)
- Ice cubes (optional)

Instructions:

1. In a blender, combine frozen peach slices, banana, Greek yogurt, peach jam, and almond milk.
2. Blend until smooth and creamy.
3. Add ice cubes if a colder consistency is desired and blend again.
4. Pour into a glass and enjoy this refreshing peach jam smoothie.

These refreshing beverages with peach jam are perfect for hot summer days or any time you crave a fruity and delightful drink. If you have a preference or need more beverage ideas, feel free to let me know! Cheers to these peachy delights.

Chapter (13) Healthier Options: Peach Jam in Light Dishes

A. Grilled Peach Jam Chicken Skewers
  Ingredients:

- 1 lb boneless, skinless chicken breasts, cut into chunks
- Salt and pepper to taste
- 1/2 cup peach jam
- 2 tablespoons soy sauce
- 1 tablespoon olive oil
- 1 teaspoon minced garlic
- Wooden skewers, soaked in water

Instructions:

1. Season chicken chunks with salt and pepper.
2. In a bowl, mix peach jam, soy sauce, olive oil, and minced garlic to create the marinade.
3. Thread chicken onto soaked wooden skewers.
4. Brush the skewers with the peach jam marinade.
5. Preheat the grill to medium-high heat.
6. Grill the skewers for 8-10 minutes, turning occasionally and brushing with more marinade.
7. Serve hot and enjoy these deliciously sweet and savory chicken skewers.

B. Peach Jam Glazed Salmon
  Ingredients:

- 4 salmon fillets

- Salt and pepper to taste
- 1/2 cup peach jam
- 2 tablespoons balsamic vinegar
- 1 tablespoon Dijon mustard
- 1 teaspoon grated ginger
- Chopped fresh parsley for garnish

Instructions:

1. Preheat the oven to 375°F (190°C).
2. Season salmon fillets with salt and pepper and place them on a baking sheet.
3. In a bowl, mix peach jam, balsamic vinegar, Dijon mustard, and grated ginger to create the glaze.
4. Brush the salmon fillets with the peach jam glaze.
5. Bake in the preheated oven for 12-15 minutes or until the salmon is cooked through.
6. Garnish with chopped fresh parsley before serving.

C. Peach Jam Quinoa Salad
Ingredients:

- 1 cup quinoa, cooked and cooled
- 1 cup cucumber, diced
- 1 cup cherry tomatoes, halved
- 1/2 cup red onion, finely chopped
- 1/4 cup feta cheese, crumbled
- 1/4 cup fresh basil, chopped
- 1/4 cup peach jam
- 2 tablespoons extra-virgin olive oil
- Salt and pepper to taste

Instructions:

1. In a large bowl, combine cooked quinoa, cucumber, cherry tomatoes, red onion, feta cheese, and fresh basil.
2. In a small bowl, whisk together peach jam, olive oil, salt, and pepper to create the dressing.
3. Pour the dressing over the quinoa mixture and toss gently to coat.
4. Chill in the refrigerator for at least 30 minutes before serving.
5. Serve as a refreshing and nutritious peach jam quinoa salad.

These healthier options incorporate the sweet and tangy flavor of peach jam into light and wholesome dishes. If you have a preference or need more healthy meal ideas, feel free to let me know! Enjoy these delightful and nutritious recipes.

Chapter (14) Seasonal Surprises: Peach Jam for Every Occasion

A. Summer Peach Jam Sorbet

Ingredients:

- 3 cups ripe peaches, peeled and diced
- 1 cup peach jam
- 1/2 cup water
- 1/4 cup fresh lemon juice
- 1/2 cup granulated sugar (adjust to taste)
- Mint leaves for garnish

Instructions:

1. In a blender, combine ripe peaches, peach jam, water, lemon juice, and granulated sugar.
2. Blend until smooth.
3. Pour the mixture into an ice cream maker and churn according to the manufacturer's instructions.
4. Transfer the sorbet to a lidded container and freeze for a few hours until firm.
5. Scoop and serve in bowls or cones.
6. Garnish with fresh mint leaves for a delightful summer treat.

B. Fall Harvest Peach Jam Pie
Ingredients:

- 1 pre-made pie crust (or homemade)
- 4 cups fresh or frozen sliced peaches
- 1 cup peach jam
- 1/2 cup granulated sugar
- 1/4 cup all-purpose flour
- 1 teaspoon ground cinnamon
- 1/4 teaspoon nutmeg
- 1 tablespoon lemon juice
- Egg wash (1 egg beaten with a splash of water)

Instructions:

1. Preheat the oven to 375°F (190°C).
2. In a large bowl, combine sliced peaches, peach jam, granulated sugar, flour, cinnamon, nutmeg, and lemon juice.
3. Roll out the pie crust and place it in a pie dish.
4. Pour the peach mixture into the pie crust.
5. Roll out the second pie crust and place it over the peach filling. Seal the edges and cut slits in the top crust for ventilation.
6. Brush the top crust with egg wash for a golden finish.
7. Bake for 40-45 minutes or until the crust is golden and the filling is bubbly.
8. Allow the pie to cool before slicing and serving.

C. Winter Spiced Peach Jam Muffins
Ingredients:

- 2 cups all-purpose flour
- 1/2 cup granulated sugar
- 2 teaspoons baking powder
- 1/2 teaspoon baking soda
- 1/2 teaspoon salt
- 1 teaspoon ground cinnamon
- 1/2 teaspoon ground nutmeg
- 1 cup buttermilk
- 1/2 cup peach jam
- 1/4 cup unsalted butter, melted
- 1 large egg
- 1 teaspoon vanilla extract

Instructions:

1. Preheat the oven to 375°F (190°C) and line a muffin tin with paper liners.
2. In a large bowl, whisk together flour, sugar, baking powder, baking soda, salt, cinnamon, and nutmeg.
3. In another bowl, mix buttermilk, peach jam, melted butter, egg, and vanilla extract.
4. Pour the wet ingredients into the dry ingredients and stir until just combined.
5. Spoon the batter into the muffin cups, filling each about 2/3 full.
6. Bake for 18-20 minutes or until a toothpick inserted into the center comes out clean.
7. Allow the muffins to cool before serving.

These seasonal surprises showcase the versatility of peach jam, bringing its delightful flavor to every occasion. Whether it's a refreshing sorbet in summer, a comforting pie in fall, or spiced muffins in winter, peach jam adds a special touch to your seasonal celebrations. If you have a preference or need more seasonal ideas, feel free to let me know! Enjoy these delightful treats throughout the year.

Chapter (15) Kids in the Kitchen: Peach Jam Fun for All Ages

A. Easy Peach Jam Sandwiches
Ingredients:

- Bread slices
- Peanut butter (or almond butter for nut-free option)
- Peach jam

Instructions:

1. Spread a layer of peanut butter on one side of a bread slice.
2. Spread peach jam on one side of another bread slice.
3. Press the two slices together with the spreads facing each other to make a sandwich.
4. Optionally, use cookie cutters to cut the sandwiches into fun shapes.

Note: Ensure the peanut butter is allowed if making these for a school setting due to allergies.

B. Peach Jam Thumbprint Art Cookies
Ingredients:

- Sugar cookie dough (pre-made or homemade)
- Peach jam
- Assorted food coloring

Instructions:

1. Preheat the oven according to the cookie dough instructions.
2. Roll the cookie dough into small balls and place them on a baking sheet.

3. Use your thumb or the back of a spoon to create an indentation in each cookie.
4. Fill each indentation with different colors of peach jam to create edible thumbprint art.
5. Bake the cookies according to the package or recipe instructions.
6. Allow them to cool before enjoying your delicious and colorful creations.

C. DIY Peach Jam Popsicles
Ingredients:

- 2 cups peach jam
- 2 cups vanilla yogurt
- Popsicle molds
- Popsicle sticks

Instructions:

1. In a bowl, mix peach jam and vanilla yogurt until well combined.
2. Spoon the mixture into popsicle molds.
3. Insert popsicle sticks into each mold.
4. Freeze the popsicles for at least 4-6 hours or until completely set.
5. Run warm water over the molds to release the popsicles easily.
6. Enjoy these homemade peach jam popsicles as a refreshing treat!

Engage kids in the kitchen with these easy and fun peach jam recipes. Whether making sandwiches, decorating cookies, or creating popsicles, these activities are sure to be a hit with the little ones. If you have a preference or need more kid-friendly ideas, feel free to let me know! Happy cooking and crafting with the kids!

Chapter (16) Homestead Harmony: Growing and Harvesting Your Own Peaches

A. Peach Tree Planting and Care

1. Selecting and Planting:

Choose a suitable peach tree variety for your climate and soil type.

Plant the tree in a location with well-draining soil and full sunlight.

Dig a hole twice as wide as the root ball and plant the tree at the same depth it was in the nursery.

2. Watering:

Water the newly planted tree thoroughly, and maintain a consistent watering schedule.

Ensure the soil is kept consistently moist, especially during dry periods.

Mulch around the base of the tree to retain moisture and suppress weeds.

3. Pruning:

Prune the tree in late winter or early spring to remove dead or damaged branches.

Create an open canopy to allow sunlight and air circulation.

Thin out excess fruit to promote larger, healthier peaches.

4. Fertilizing:

Apply a balanced fertilizer in early spring before new growth begins.

Follow the recommended dosage based on the tree's age and size.

Avoid over-fertilizing, as it can lead to excessive foliage growth at the expense of fruit.

B. Harvesting Peaches at the Peak of Ripeness

1. Determining Ripeness:

Assess the color of the peaches; they should have a vibrant, well-developed hue.

Gently squeeze the peaches; they should yield slightly without being too soft.

Smell the fruit; ripe peaches have a sweet and fragrant aroma.

2. Harvesting Technique:

Use pruning shears to cut the peaches from the tree, leaving a small stem attached.

Handle the peaches carefully to avoid bruising.

Harvest when the peaches are fully colored but still slightly firm.

3. Timing:

Harvest peaches when they are at their peak ripeness, usually in late spring to early summer.

Check individual varieties for specific harvesting times.

C. Preserving the Harvest Beyond Jam

1. Peach Preserves:

Make peach preserves by cooking peeled and sliced peaches with sugar until thickened.

Add lemon juice for acidity and flavor enhancement.

Store in sterilized jars for long-term preservation.

2. Peach Salsa:

Create a savory peach salsa with diced peaches, tomatoes, onions, cilantro, lime juice, and a touch of jalapeño.

Enjoy it fresh or can it for extended shelf life.

3. Freeze for Later Use:

Slice peeled peaches and freeze them on a baking sheet before transferring to freezer bags.

Use frozen peaches in smoothies, desserts, or thaw for a refreshing snack.

4. Dehydrated Peach Chips:

Slice peaches thinly and dehydrate them until they reach a crisp texture.

Store in airtight containers for a healthy and delicious snack.

Harvesting and preserving your own peaches is a rewarding experience that allows you to enjoy the fruits of your labor in various culinary creations beyond traditional jam. If you have specific questions or need more tips on peach cultivation, feel free to ask! Happy homesteading!

Chapter (17) Gourmet Pairings: Peach Jam with Cheese and More

A. Peach Jam and Brie Crostini
   Ingredients:

- Baguette, sliced
- Brie cheese, sliced
- Peach jam
- Fresh thyme leaves for garnish

Instructions:

1. Preheat the oven broiler.
2. Place baguette slices on a baking sheet and toast under the broiler until lightly golden.
3. Place a slice of Brie on each toasted baguette slice.
4. Spoon a small amount of peach jam on top of the Brie.
5. Place the crostinis back under the broiler for a minute or until the Brie is melted.
6. Garnish with fresh thyme leaves and serve immediately.

B. Peach Jam Cheese Board Pairings
Cheese Board Ingredients:

- Assorted cheeses (Brie, Camembert, Gouda, blue cheese)
- Crackers or baguette slices
- Peach jam
- Nuts (walnuts, almonds)
- Fresh or dried fruits (grapes, figs, apricots)
- Honey for drizzling
- Fresh herbs for garnish

Instructions:

1. Arrange a variety of cheeses on a cheese board.
2. Place crackers or baguette slices alongside the cheeses.
3. Spoon peach jam into small serving bowls and place them on the board.
4. Scatter nuts and fresh or dried fruits around the cheeses.
5. Drizzle honey over the cheeses.
6. Garnish with fresh herbs for a visually appealing presentation.
7. Allow guests to create their own perfect bites.

C. Peach Jam and Prosciutto Wrapped Appetizers
Ingredients:

- Slices of prosciutto
- Fresh mozzarella balls
- Basil leaves
- Peach jam

Instructions:

1. Lay out slices of prosciutto.
2. Place a fresh mozzarella ball and a basil leaf at one end of each prosciutto slice.
3. Roll the prosciutto around the mozzarella and basil, creating small appetizer bundles.
4. Arrange the bundles on a serving platter.
5. Spoon a dollop of peach jam on top of each bundle.
6. Serve these elegant and flavorful appetizers at your next gathering.

These gourmet pairings with peach jam elevate the culinary experience, adding a sweet and savory twist to classic combinations. Whether served on crostinis, incorporated into a cheese board, or wrapped in prosciutto, these creations are sure to impress. If you have specific preferences or need more gourmet pairing ideas, feel free to let me know! Enjoy these delightful and sophisticated flavors.

Chapter (18) International Sweets: Peach Jam Desserts from Around the World

A. Italian Peach Jam Tiramisu
Ingredients:

- Ladyfinger cookies (Savoiardi)
- 1 cup strong brewed coffee, cooled
- 3 tablespoons peach jam
- 1 cup mascarpone cheese
- 1/2 cup granulated sugar
- 1 teaspoon vanilla extract
- Cocoa powder for dusting

Instructions:

1. In a bowl, mix mascarpone cheese, sugar, and vanilla extract until smooth.
2. In a separate shallow dish, combine brewed coffee and peach jam.
3. Dip each ladyfinger into the coffee and jam mixture, ensuring they are coated but not soggy.
4. Arrange a layer of soaked ladyfingers in a serving dish.
5. Spread a layer of the mascarpone mixture over the ladyfingers.
6. Repeat the layers, finishing with a layer of mascarpone on top.
7. Refrigerate for at least 4 hours or overnight.
8. Dust with cocoa powder before serving.

B. French Peach Jam Tart
Ingredients:

- 1 pre-made pie crust (or homemade)
- 1 cup peach jam
- 1/2 cup almond flour
- 3 eggs
- 1/2 cup unsalted butter, melted
- Sliced almonds for garnish

Instructions:

1. Preheat the oven to 350°F (175°C).
2. Roll out the pie crust and place it in a tart pan.
3. In a bowl, mix peach jam, almond flour, eggs, and melted butter until well combined.
4. Pour the mixture into the tart crust.
5. Bake for 30-35 minutes or until the filling is set and golden.
6. Allow the tart to cool before garnishing with sliced almonds.

C. Greek Yogurt Parfait with Peach Jam

Ingredients:

- Greek yogurt
- Granola
- Fresh sliced peaches
- Peach jam
- Honey for drizzling

Instructions:

1. In a glass or bowl, layer Greek yogurt, granola, and fresh sliced peaches.
2. Add a spoonful of peach jam on top of each layer.
3. Repeat the layers until the glass is filled.
4. Drizzle with honey if desired.
5. Serve immediately and enjoy this delightful Greek-inspired

parfait.

Indulge in the sweetness of international desserts with these peach jam-inspired creations. Whether it's the classic Italian Tiramisu, a French Peach Jam Tart, or a Greek Yogurt Parfait, these recipes bring a touch of global flair to your dessert table. If you have specific preferences or need more international dessert ideas, feel free to let me know! Bon appétit!

Chapter (19) Jam-Making Traditions: Peach Jam in Family and Cultural Celebrations

A. Incorporating Peach Jam in Family Recipes

1. Peach Jam-Stuffed Pastries:

Use peach jam as a filling for traditional family pastries or turnovers.

Incorporate it into recipes passed down through generations.

2. Peach Jam Glazed Meat Dishes:

Create a family-favorite glaze using peach jam for meats like ham, chicken, or pork.

Infuse your family's special touch into classic savory dishes.

3. Signature Peach Jam Cocktails:

Develop a signature family cocktail by incorporating peach jam into drinks.

Serve these refreshing beverages during family gatherings and celebrations.

B. Peach Jam-Making Traditions Around the World

1. Japanese Mochi with Peach Jam:

Embrace the Japanese tradition of making mochi filled with peach jam.

Celebrate special occasions with these delicate and sweet treats.

2. Spanish Peach Jam Churros:

Integrate the Spanish love for churros by serving them with a peach jam dipping sauce.

Enjoy this fusion of flavors in cultural celebrations.

3. Indian Peach Jam Lassi:

Infuse the richness of Indian cuisine by incorporating peach jam into a traditional lassi.

Share this delightful and exotic beverage during festive occasions.

C. Creating New Peach Jam Traditions

1. Annual Peach Jam-Making Day:

Establish a yearly tradition where family and friends gather to make peach jam together.

Share stories, laughter, and create lasting memories during this special day.

2. Peach Jam Recipe Exchange:

Initiate a recipe exchange within the family or community, focusing on different ways to use peach jam.

Compile a cookbook that becomes a cherished family heirloom.

3. Peach Jam Tasting Event:

Organize a peach jam tasting event where everyone brings their unique peach jam creations.

Vote on favorites and crown the "Peach Jam Connoisseur" of the year.

By incorporating peach jam into family recipes, exploring jam-making traditions from around the world, and creating new peach jam traditions, you contribute to the rich tapestry of culinary heritage.

Celebrate the versatility of peach jam in family and cultural celebrations, fostering a sense of connection and joy. If you have specific preferences or need more ideas for creating peach jam traditions, feel free to let me know! Cheers to the delightful traditions centered around peach jam!

Chapter (20) Culinary Adventures: Peach Jam in Fusion Cuisine

A. Peach Jam Sushi Rolls
   Ingredients:

- Nori (seaweed) sheets
- Sushi rice
- Fresh slices of peach
- Avocado slices
- Cream cheese
- Crab or shrimp (optional)
- Soy sauce for dipping

Instructions:

1. Place a sheet of nori on a bamboo sushi rolling mat.
2. Spread a layer of sushi rice evenly over the nori, leaving a small border at the top.
3. Arrange slices of peach, avocado, cream cheese, and any optional seafood along the bottom edge of the rice.
4. Roll the sushi tightly using the bamboo mat, sealing the edge with a little water.
5. Slice the roll into bite-sized pieces.
6. Serve with soy sauce for dipping.

B. Tex-Mex Peach Jam Quesadillas

Ingredients:

- Flour tortillas
- Shredded cooked chicken
- Peach jam
- Shredded cheddar cheese
- Jalapeño slices (optional)
- Fresh cilantro, chopped
- Sour cream for dipping

Instructions:

1. Place a tortilla on a heated skillet or griddle.
2. Spread a layer of peach jam on one half of the tortilla.
3. Add shredded chicken, cheddar cheese, jalapeño slices, and chopped cilantro.
4. Fold the tortilla in half, pressing gently with a spatula.
5. Cook until the cheese is melted and the tortilla is golden brown on both sides.
6. Repeat with additional tortillas.
7. Slice into wedges and serve with sour cream.

C. Peach Jam Fusion Tacos

Ingredients:

- Soft corn or flour tortillas
- Grilled shrimp or chicken
- Cabbage slaw (shredded cabbage, carrots, and lime vinaigrette)
- Peach jam
- Crumbled queso fresco or feta cheese
- Fresh cilantro, chopped

Instructions:

1. Grill shrimp or chicken until fully cooked.
2. Warm tortillas on a skillet or in the oven.
3. Spread a layer of peach jam on each tortilla.
4. Top with grilled shrimp or chicken.
5. Add a generous portion of cabbage slaw on top.
6. Sprinkle crumbled queso fresco or feta cheese.
7. Garnish with chopped cilantro.
8. Serve these Peach Jam Fusion Tacos with a squeeze of lime.

Embark on a culinary adventure with these fusion cuisine creations featuring the unique and delightful addition of peach jam. Whether it's in sushi rolls, quesadillas, or tacos, the sweet and savory fusion will surely surprise and delight your taste buds. If you have specific preferences or need more fusion cuisine ideas, feel free to let me know! Enjoy these innovative and flavorful dishes.

Chapter (21) Artisanal Jam-Making Techniques

A. Small-Batch Peach Jam

Ingredients:

- 4 cups fresh peaches, peeled and diced
- 2 cups granulated sugar
- 1 lemon, juiced
- 1 package (1.75 oz) fruit pectin
- Optional: 1 vanilla bean, scraped for seeds

Instructions:

1. In a large pot, combine diced peaches, sugar, and lemon juice.
2. Mash the peaches slightly to release their juices.
3. If using, add the vanilla bean seeds to the mixture.
4. Bring the mixture to a boil over medium heat, stirring frequently.
5. Stir in the fruit pectin, ensuring it's well incorporated.
6. Boil for 1-2 minutes until the jam thickens.
7. Skim off any foam from the top.
8. Ladle the hot jam into sterilized jars, leaving a quarter-inch headspace.
9. Seal the jars and process them in a hot water bath for preservation.
10. Allow the jars to cool completely before storing.

Note: Adjust sugar quantity based on your preference and the sweetness of the peaches.

B. Infusing Flavors with Herbs and Spices
Ingredients:

- Basic Peach Jam (from the small-batch recipe)
- Herbs: Fresh basil, mint, or thyme (choose one)
- Spices: Cinnamon sticks, star anise, or ginger (choose one)

Instructions:

1. Prepare the basic peach jam following the small-batch recipe.
2. In the last 5 minutes of cooking, add a handful of fresh herbs or a spice of your choice to infuse flavor.
3. Remove the herbs or spices before ladling the jam into jars for preservation.

Note: Experiment with different herb and spice combinations to create unique flavor profiles.

C. Aging and Maturing Peach Jam
Ingredients:

- Basic Peach Jam (from the small-batch recipe)

Instructions:

1. Prepare the basic peach jam following the small-batch recipe.
2. Allow the jam to cool completely in the jars before sealing them.
3. Store the sealed jars in a cool, dark place for at least one month, allowing the flavors to meld and intensify.
4. After aging, taste the jam and adjust sweetness or add more flavors if desired.
5. Store the jam in the refrigerator after opening.

Note: Aging time can vary based on personal preference, but a month is a good starting point.

These artisanal jam-making techniques add a personal touch to your peach jam, allowing you to experiment with small batches, infuse unique flavors, and even age the jam for a more developed taste. Whether you choose to make a small-batch for immediate enjoyment, infuse herbs and spices for a distinctive flavor, or age the jam for a matured taste, these techniques elevate the art of jam-making. If you have specific preferences or need more artisanal jam-making ideas, feel free to let me know! Enjoy the process of creating your own signature peach jam.

Chapter (22) Sustainable Jam-Making Practices

A. Ethical Sourcing of Ingredients

1. Local and Organic Peaches:

Source peaches from local farmers or farmers' markets to reduce the carbon footprint.

Choose organic peaches to support sustainable farming practices.

2. Fair Trade Sugar:

Opt for fair trade-certified sugar to ensure fair wages and ethical treatment of workers.

3. Responsible Pectin Choice:

Select fruit pectin brands that prioritize sustainable and ethical sourcing of ingredients.

B. Zero-Waste Jam-Making Tips

1. Composting Peels and Pits:

Compost peach peels and pits instead of discarding them in the trash.

2. Reusable Utensils and Equipment:

Use reusable utensils and equipment during the jam-making process to reduce single-use plastic waste.

3. Preserve Excess Peaches:

If you have more peaches than needed, consider preserving them in different ways (canning, freezing) to minimize food waste.

4. Homemade Fruit Pectin:

Make your own fruit pectin from apple scraps or citrus peels to avoid commercial pectin packaging.

C. Eco-Friendly Packaging Ideas

1. Reusable Jars:

Use reusable glass jars for storing peach jam. Mason jars are excellent for this purpose.

2. Beeswax Wraps or Cloth Covers:

Instead of using plastic wrap, cover jars with beeswax wraps or cloth secured with twine for a charming, eco-friendly touch.

3. Biodegradable Labels:

If labeling jars, opt for biodegradable or recyclable labels.

4. Gift Packaging with a Purpose:

When gifting peach jam, use sustainable packaging such as reusable fabric wraps or eco-friendly gift bags.

5. Upcycled Jam Jar Crafts:

Encourage recipients to upcycle the empty jam jars into creative crafts or storage containers.

By incorporating ethical ingredient sourcing, practicing zero-waste jam-making techniques, and utilizing eco-friendly packaging, you can contribute to sustainable and environmentally conscious jam-making. These practices not only minimize your environmental impact but also add an extra layer of thoughtfulness to your homemade peach jam. If you have specific preferences or need more sustainable jam-making ideas, feel free to let me know! Enjoy making delicious peach jam while caring for the planet.

Chapter (23) Beyond the Jar: Peach Jam in DIY Beauty Products

A. Peach Jam Lip Balm
Ingredients:

- 1 tablespoon peach jam (strained to remove solids)
- 1 tablespoon coconut oil
- 1 tablespoon beeswax pellets
- 1 teaspoon honey
- Empty lip balm containers

Instructions:

1. In a heatproof bowl, combine peach jam, coconut oil, beeswax pellets, and honey.
2. Place the bowl over a pot of simmering water (double boiler) and stir until the ingredients melt and blend.
3. Remove from heat and carefully pour the mixture into empty lip balm containers.
4. Let it cool and solidify before capping the containers.
5. Apply your peach-infused lip balm for a sweet and moisturizing touch.

B. Peach Jam Sugar Scrub
Ingredients:

- 1/2 cup granulated sugar
- 2 tablespoons peach jam
- 2 tablespoons coconut oil
- 1 teaspoon vanilla extract (optional)

Instructions:

1. In a bowl, combine granulated sugar, peach jam, coconut oil, and vanilla extract.
2. Mix the ingredients thoroughly until you achieve a scrub-like consistency.
3. Use the peach jam sugar scrub in the shower by gently massaging it onto damp skin.
4. Rinse off to reveal soft and exfoliated skin with a hint of peachy sweetness.

C. Peach Jam Hair Mask
Ingredients:

- 3 tablespoons peach jam
- 2 tablespoons plain yogurt
- 1 tablespoon honey
- 1 tablespoon olive oil

Instructions:

1. Mix peach jam, yogurt, honey, and olive oil in a bowl until well combined.
2. Apply the mixture to damp hair, focusing on the ends and avoiding the roots.
3. Cover your hair with a shower cap and let the mask sit for 30-60 minutes.
4. Rinse thoroughly with shampoo and conditioner.
5. Enjoy soft, nourished hair with a subtle peach fragrance.

Beyond the jar, explore the beauty-enhancing qualities of peach jam with these simple DIY recipes. From luscious lip balm to rejuvenating sugar scrub and a nourishing hair mask, let the natural goodness of peaches elevate your beauty routine. If you have specific preferences or need more DIY beauty product ideas, feel free to let me know! Pamper yourself with the delightful essence of peach in these homemade beauty treats.

Chapter (24) Virtual Peach Jam Community: Online Sharing and Collaborations

A. Joining Online Jam-Making Communities

1. Social Media Groups:

Connect with fellow jam enthusiasts on platforms like Facebook, Instagram, or Pinterest.

Share your peach jam journey, exchange tips, and discover new recipes.

2. Online Forums:

Explore dedicated jam-making forums where you can seek advice, troubleshoot issues, and celebrate successes with a global community of jam makers.

3. Recipe Platforms:

Join recipe-sharing websites like Allrecipes or Food.com to exchange peach jam recipes, variations, and experiences.

B. Hosting Virtual Jam-Making Parties

1. Live Streaming Sessions:

Use platforms like Zoom or YouTube to host live jam-making sessions.

Invite friends and family to join virtually, sharing the joy of peach jam-making in real-time.

2. Collaborative Recipe Creation:

Plan virtual jam-making parties where participants contribute unique ingredients or variations to a collective recipe.

Discuss techniques, troubleshoot together, and end the session with a diverse array of peach jams.

3. Online Jam-Making Challenges:

Organize friendly challenges with online friends to create the most innovative peach jam using surprise ingredients.

Share the results and experiences on social media for others to enjoy.

C. Collaborative Peach Jam Recipes from Around the Web

1. Recipe Exchanges:

Collaborate with fellow bloggers or online platforms to exchange and feature each other's peach jam recipes.

Provide links to diverse recipes to offer a comprehensive guide for your virtual community.

2. Guest Contributions:

Invite guest contributors to share their favorite peach jam recipes on your blog or platform.

Encourage a sense of community by showcasing different perspectives and flavor profiles.

3. Interactive Recipe Polls:

Conduct polls or surveys to gather input from your online community about their favorite peach jam flavor combinations.

Turn the most popular suggestions into collaborative recipes.

Embrace the digital age by becoming a part of the virtual peach jam community. Joining online groups, hosting virtual jam-making parties, and collaborating on recipes from around the web create a vibrant and inclusive space for jam enthusiasts. Share your experiences, learn from others, and let the collective passion for peach jam-making flourish in the online world. If you have specific preferences or need more ideas for online collaborations, feel free to let me know! Connect, create, and enjoy the virtual peach jam journey together.

Chapter (25) Peach Jam for Special Diets

A. Sugar-Free Peach Jam for Diabetics
Ingredients:

- 4 cups fresh peaches, peeled and diced
- 1 cup water
- 1 packet no-sugar-needed fruit pectin
- Stevia or monk fruit sweetener to taste

Instructions:

1. In a pot, combine diced peaches and water. Simmer until peaches are soft.
2. Mash the peaches to your desired consistency.
3. Stir in the no-sugar-needed fruit pectin and sweeten with stevia or monk fruit, adjusting to taste.
4. Bring the mixture to a boil and cook for 1-2 minutes until it thickens.
5. Ladle the sugar-free peach jam into sterilized jars and seal.

Note: Adjust sweetener to your preference and consider the natural sweetness of peaches.

B. Vegan-Friendly Peach Jam Recipes

1. Basic Vegan Peach Jam:

Follow the classic peach jam recipe, substituting agar-agar or pectin suitable for vegans.

Ensure the sugar used is vegan-friendly, avoiding bone-char processed sugar.

2. Peach and Chia Seed Jam:

Combine 4 cups diced peaches, 1/4 cup chia seeds, and sweetener of choice.

Let the mixture sit for 30 minutes to allow chia seeds to gel.

Adjust sweetness and blend for a smoother consistency if desired.

3. Spiced Vegan Peach Jam:

Add a dash of cinnamon, nutmeg, and a pinch of salt to the basic vegan peach jam for a delightful spiced version.

C. Gluten-Free Peach Jam Treats

1. Gluten-Free Peach Jam Thumbprint Cookies:

Use a gluten-free cookie base, create an indentation with your thumb, and fill with your favorite peach jam.

2. Gluten-Free Peach Jam Swirl Ice Cream:

Swirl peach jam into a base of gluten-free vanilla ice cream for a refreshing and gluten-free frozen treat.

3. Gluten-Free Peach Jam Cheesecake Bars:

Make a gluten-free crust using almond flour or gluten-free graham crackers for the cheesecake bars.

Swirl peach jam into the cheesecake batter before baking.

❖ Conclusion

A. Celebrating the Joy of Peach Jam-Making

Embarking on the journey of peach jam-making is not just a culinary endeavor; it's a celebration of flavors, traditions, and creativity. The process of transforming fresh, juicy peaches into a delightful spread offers a sense of accomplishment and a connection to nature's bounty. Whether you're a seasoned jam-maker or a newcomer to the art, the joy lies in the aroma that fills your kitchen, the vibrant colors that dance in your jars, and the satisfaction of creating something truly special.

As you savor the sweet and versatile results of your peach jam-making, take a moment to appreciate the tradition, innovation, and love that went into each jar. From classic recipes to international twists, from family traditions to culinary adventures, each batch reflects a unique blend of your preferences, creativity, and the spirit of sharing.

B. Share Your Peach Jam Adventures

The beauty of peach jam-making extends beyond the confines of your kitchen. It's an opportunity to share the love and flavors with family, friends, and even your community. Whether you create personalized gift baskets, share jars with neighbors, or host a peach jam-tasting event, spreading the joy is an integral part of the experience.

Share your peach jam adventures on social media, swap recipes with fellow jam enthusiasts, and inspire others to embark on their own fruity journeys. Whether you choose to preserve the traditions, infuse innovative flavors, or explore sustainable practices, your peach jam-making endeavors contribute to a tapestry of shared experiences that transcend borders and cultures.

So, in the spirit of peachy delights, celebrate the joy of creating, sharing, and savoring every spoonful of your homemade peach jam. Whether it's enjoyed on a lazy Sunday morning, shared during festive gatherings, or given as a thoughtful gift, your peach jam is a testament to the artistry and passion that flavors life's sweet moments. Cheers to the delightful world of peach jam-making!